52 WEEKS
OF WISDOM

An Essential Guide to
Effective Leadership

David P. Robinson, Ph.D.

City Limits International Publishing

Chicago, IL 2019

"Your Mission is Our Motivation...
Your Success is Our Inspiration"

52 Weeks of Wisdom, an essential guide to effective leadership

Copyright © by David P. Robinson, Ph.D.

All Rights Reserved

ISBN 9781092766517
Cover designed and created by Steven Sisler

First Edition, April 2019
Printed in the United States of America

Other books and leadership materials may be ordered through booksellers or contacting:

City Limits International
PO Box 6086
Elgin IL 60121
www.coaching4ministers.com
www.transformingyourcity.com

Dedication

To my wife, Marie, the light of my life and love of my heart!

Your faithful support keeps me going.

CONTENTS

ENDORSEMENTS

"We have worked with David Robinson, Sr. for a number of years in the RV Industry. In all of our dealings with him, we have found him to be honest and trustworthy. Mr. Robinson took over a troubled dealership and has worked hard to turn things around. And, in the process, he has lived up to every agreement made with us. Not only is David Robinson, Sr. a man of integrity, but he is also a pleasure to work with. We would not hesitate to recommend him for any type of business undertaking."

Kay L. Toolson
Chief Executive Officer/Chairman Monaco Coach Corporation
Coburg, OR

"I have known David Robinson, Sr., for 5 to 6 years, since the time he, along with minority investors, purchased an RV (recreational vehicle) dealership in Illinois. This dealership had failed under the previous owners and faced dual challenges of a less than optimal business location and product mix. Nonetheless, David worked hard to create a viable business which continues to operate to this day. I consider him to be a man of honor and high personal integrity. I always found David to be accessible, frank, direct, and open in our discussions. He always conveyed a strong sense of wanting to conduct his relationships (whether with customers or business associates) in an ethical manner. I grew to respect him very much and was sorry to see him sell his ownership in the business."

James R. Hamel
Vice President–Operations GE Commercial Finance/Home & Recreational Vehicle Group
Tempe AZ

"I have had the privilege of working with as our leadership coach for the past 2 years. In all my interactions with David, I have been impressed with his creative coaching skills and professionalism. I am completely satisfied with David's method of coaching and value added to our leadership team. I am, therefore, pleased to endorse David, without reservation."

Gary W. Passero
CEO PASSERO ASSOCIATES ENGINEERING
Rochester, NY

"David is highly skilled at integrating sound principles and both practical and strategic thinking with realistic planning to achieve pre-agreed upon goals. He is a gifted manager and planner who "walks the walk" and practices what he teaches. His consistency of attitude, word and strength is inspirational. Moreover, David is a frank mentor, completely engaged to help find all possible options, help you identify and evaluate them and go with the one that best fits all stated (usually written) objectives using high standards and identified skill sets for individuals or teams or both. His work may serve to show you that reevaluation of and focus upon project goals or current organizational talent and infrastructure, or both, will lead to identifying relevant, worthwhile, and practical changes.

Geoffrey Hichborn
Sr. Chief Engineer and Lead Consultant at Building Forensics International
Anaheim CA

INTRODUCTION
"Solving Problems or Creating the Future"

Are you solving problems or creating the future? There are two basic kinds of leaders; those who solve daily management problems and those who provide strategic leadership. Both are vital for success. It always works best if the senior leader has strategic planning skills. If not, the organization, gets bogged down in management challenges, forward momentum slows, pursuit of the vision is non-existent and active inertia sets in.

Strategic planning is hard work. It requires objective and sometimes painful looks in the mirror. Without defining present reality with brutal honesty, you are not ready for the future. Many leadership teams are hesitant to challenge the status quo, change behaviors, or execute new procedures. Why? Because, *"that's the way we have always done it"* remains the most comfortable leadership style and nothing changes. The pace of today's changing world and the need to remain relevant demands an on-going strategic planning process and rigorous execution by the leadership team.

If you are a senior leader or serve on a core leadership team, strategic planning must be a core value and your primary function. If not, you should move to the management team because chances are you are a problem solver and function better managing the future that others create.

What about your organization, ministry or marketplace effort? Do you focus more on today's problems, or tomorrow's opportunities? Do you have a strategy (action plan) that is clear to everyone on your team? Does everyone know the current goals and how they will be achieved? Does your structure bring operational value on a daily basis? Do the behaviors of your team members align with your values, goals and strategy?

Why is strategic planning so important? It is if growth and fulfilling your vision is important. Leaders who say they have a vision but cannot adequately define it amaze me because they have no defined action plan to get there. Strategic planning brings objectivity and structure to the planning process. It sets the stage and guides the leadership team in a common and focused direction. It provides a road map for success.

Strategic planning directs the investment of resources and provides accountability for results. It's a great way to measure success and return on investment. A good strategic plan, properly executed, accomplishes the following seven things:

1. Brings clarity on mission, vision and values.

2. Helps in planning efforts and improve the decision-making process.

3. Helps anticipate and manage change.

4. Aligns everyone's priorities and purpose.

5. Establishes performance expectations and identify strengths and weaknesses.

6. Critiques systems and processes.

7. Creates and maintains a culture of constant improvement.

Organizations that perform at the highest levels of achievement, while maintaining a spirit of excellence, do so because they stay engaged in a good strategic planning process. Conversely, a leading cause of organizational failure is the lack of adequate long-range planning tools executed consistently.

Strategic planning, along with many other leadership challenges, always goes better with an outside facilitator or coach. Why do they help things go better?

1. They bring objectivity and structure to the process.

2. They bring a sense of urgency to the real issues.

3. They help clarify and merge competing priorities.

4. They help identify and eliminate non-productive behaviors.

5. They challenge assumptions and the status quo.

6. They provide options not previously considered.

7. They help leaders stay focused on solutions--not just problems.

You can create a better today with better management solutions; however, you can only create a better tomorrow through better strategic planning and rigorous execution. As a senior leader, what is your priority? "Here are 52 leadership thoughts that will help you succeed in your leadership challenges."

"Developing passionate leaders, building energized teams and finding sustainable solutions since 1966"

Week 1

"Here lies a man, who knew how to enlist in his service better men than himself"

Growing up in Western Pennsylvania near Pittsburgh I was very familiar with the name, Andrew Carnegie. I spent many hours studying for a test in one of the numerous libraries named after this nineteenth century steel magnate.

Carnegie was a great philanthropist grown from the crucible of poverty and hard work. He proclaimed in his article "The Gospel of Wealth" the belief that those who earn more have the greater responsibility for the welfare of others. He not only proclaimed it, he did it. He built libraries and academic halls all over the area around Pittsburgh.

However, perhaps Carnegie's greatest achievement is revealed in the words chiseled on his tombstone:

"Here lies a man, who knew how to enlist in his service better men than himself"

When the last words said about someone's life speak of others, you can truthfully say that person modeled servant-leadership. Yes, Carnegie enjoyed the finer things of life, but his greatest joy was seeing others succeed.

Seeing and exploiting greatness in others always separates average leaders from great leaders. Being able to compliment, nourish and strengthen someone else demonstrates that you are never alone or without meaning in your work, regardless of your vocation.

Great leaders are growers of great people. They're the people who step away from their desks, or their personal challenges when you come into view. They're the leaders who ask the tough questions, not to show how smart they are, but to show you how talented you are. Great leaders hold the flashlight and light the path forward and help you see your dream come true. Poor leaders say, "Hold the light higher I can't see where I'm going."

As a leader, hopefully bringing out the best in others is among your goals for 2018. Use your influence to make at least one other person's life significantly better this year. Don't forfeit your right to lead by thinking God created everyone else to serve you. The greater your rank simply means the bigger your mop bucket.

What will they inscribe on your tombstone?

"For even the Son of Man came to this earth to serve, not be served." Mark 10:45

"Do you know the WHY of your leadership?"

When Steve Jobs was CEO of Apple, he challenged fellow CEO, John Scully, to leave PepsiCo and join his startup company that lacked both adequate resources and name recognition.

Jobs could not offer him more money or security, but instead offered him purpose the chance to change the way the world communicates, learns and exchanges information instead of making sugar water.

What is the purpose for all the roles you play is one of life's fundamental questions? Most people work harder on the "what" and "how" questions when they should be asking why—what is the purpose?

As a leader your ability to create a compelling purpose and keep your team focused on its completion is often the difference between winning and losing. This ability above almost anything else is what separates average leaders from the great ones.

When a leader is dedicated to a purpose, the WHY, their energy and level of engagement and that of their team increases. Their dedication to winning is stronger and lasts longer. No leader ever unified the efforts of people, raised substantial resources and successfully achieved what seems impossible without an unwavering sense of purpose.

The capabilities of great leaders are more than charismatic personalities, effective communication styles and mastering the art of persuasion. These are of little value unless all team members understand the purpose, the why. Confidence comes from knowing what to do and how to do it. However, passionate engagement comes from knowing why.

Hurdles, obstacles and times of crisis test every leader's best efforts. In fact, it's these very challenges that creates the purpose for your leadership. There is no autopilot or default position for purpose. You cannot take your eye off of your purpose for long without it derailing your entire effort. Tough times is the breakfast of champion leaders, they thrive on it.

Adversity quickly stops a weak or inexperienced leader without purpose, but it only fans the flames of great leaders who don't know the meaning of can't or quit. Leadership must be more than talk. You must do everything on purpose for a purpose if you want to be a great leader.

"But this one thing I do; forgetting what is behind and straining toward what is ahead, I press toward the goal (purpose)." Philippians 3:12-14

Do those following your leadership understand the why, the purpose for who they are and what they do? How do you know? Why not ask them? Their answers may surprise you.

If your team believes in you and understands their "why," you will never lack for passionate team members.

Week 3

"3 Keys in getting to the next level."

"Management is efficiency in climbing the ladder of success; leadership determines whether the ladder is leaning against the right wall." Stephen Covey

With enough education, talent and hard work most people are considered successful, depending on what standard you use in defining success. However, you can be a success in life without fulfilling the purpose for your life. Success in life is determined by four words: purpose, potential, promises and provision.

Great leaders stay on a constant learning curve focused on those four words. In your climb to success don't forget to take your team along. Here are three keys for climbing the ladder of success, getting to the next level and fulfilling your destiny:

First, decide to change. Change begins with a made-up mind and a heart that will not accept defeat.

"If you decided to kick the person most responsible for your troubles, you would not be able to sit down for a week." G. K. Chesterton

Change the way you think, you change the way you speak. Change the way you speak, you change the way you feel. Change the way you feel, you change the way you act. Change the way you act, you change the result.

Second, great expectations. Research shows there's a greater connection between self-confidence and achievement than between I.Q. and achievement. How much more should confidence (trust) in God change our expectations? Even our U.S. coinage still carries, "In God We Trust."

If Michelangelo had consulted his doubts and critics, he would have painted the floor instead of the ceiling of the Sistine Chapel. Never let your problems, or your critics determine your level of success because neither had anything to do with determining your success or destiny.

Third, keep practicing. Charlie Brown said to Linus; "Life is too much for me. I've been confused since I was born. I think the trouble is we're thrown into life too soon." Linus asked, "What do you want?" Charlie responds, "A chance to warm up."

Practice what is important for your success before the game. Wisdom, knowledge and understanding are fundamental for success in any field. In addition, half of getting to the next level is knowing what you have to give up to get there.

"He is no fool who gives up what he cannot keep to gain what he cannot lose." Jim Elliot

Jim wrote this in his diary, October 1949 as a student at Wheaton College just a few years before he and four companions were martyred as young missionaries in Equator in 1956.

What will you have to give up to get to your next level, to fulfill your purpose?

"How to avoid being overworked and feeling overwhelmed."

Poor leaders find themselves running out of time while their direct reports lack motivation and are running out of productive work. Great leadership is not about your personal production but your team's production, especially when you are not around.

Delegation and deferring are two of your most important strengths as a leader. Doing them well is a must for providing effective leadership and significant success. Great leaders spend less time "doing" and invest most of their time planning, organizing resources and coaching their team to do the "doing."

There is a major difference between delegating and deferring. Delegating means you still own some responsibility for the results, deferring means you give the task away without any further responsibility. Great leaders use both and know when and how to use them.

Some warning signs you need to improve your delegating skills:

1. Your in-box is always full of work only YOU can do.

2. Delegated assignments are often incomplete, and deadlines missed.

3. Direct reports feel they lack authority, resources and empowerment.

4. You constantly second guess your team members' decisions.

5. Team morale is low, turnover rates rising and people lack motivation.

6. You frequently intervene in work you previously delegated or deferred.

7. Team members feel unprepared and are not taking full responsibility.

Tips for delegating effectively:

1. Recognize and affirm the capabilities of your team for their assignments.

2. Focus on results, not how tasks should be accomplished.

3. Use delegation to develop the skills of your team members and position them for advancement.

4. Always delegate or defer to the lowest level possible.

5. Explain assignments clearly and provide necessary resources.

6. Provide consistent feedback, emotional support during tough times and celebrate all wins, big or small.

7. Defer more, give away responsibility for results and avoid the comebacks.

Overworked and overwhelmed leaders are leaders who failed to learn how to delegate and defer effectively.

As a result, your best people leave you because they are bored, you hold back the development of your good people and your average team members are burned up or burned out because of trying to do it all.

How are you feeling as you start a new week?

Week 5

"What does it take to stop you?"

"Effort only fully releases its reward when you refuse to quit." Napoleon Hill

Before success comes in any persons' life, they often meet with failure and defeat. When discouragement overtakes a person the easiest and most logical thing to do is quit. That's exactly what the majority of people do, they give up when victory is knocking, and they fail to open the door.

Nothing can stop you, if:

1. You have identified your governing values. You will argue for your convictions, but you will die for your core values. What three to five core values govern your life? If you hesitate, or just do not know, then you are only a product of someone else's values. There are many valuable things you could do with your life; but great leaders are passionate about the one that rises above all others. What is yours? If you do not know, you can be stopped.

2. You have set goals that help you do something about those values. A goal is planned conflict with the status quo. To pursue a goal, you must do something new, leave the familiar, get out of your comfort zone and explore new opportunities.

3. You are determined, a made-up mind is a battle won. You persevere until you win. Someone once said, "Be like a stamp, stick to it until arriving at the predetermined destination without a return address."

Why not memorize Ella Wheeler's poem "Will" this week?

"There is no chance, no destiny, and no fate that can circumvent, or hinder, or control that firm resolve of a determined soul."

Winston Churchill said, "Success is going from failure to failure without losing enthusiasm."

The reason most people never achieve their dreams, they simply quit, they give up too soon. Life was never meant to be easy. Without struggle nothing develops, whether it's a butterfly, acorns, or you. Remember, the times when it's most important to persevere are the times that you will be most tested.

A longtime friend of mine, Mike Adkins, wrote and recorded one of my favorite songs, "Don't Give up on the Brink of a Miracle." Why not download it today on your smart phone?

You will never know how close your victory is if you quit. If you can be stopped—you will be stopped!

"If you believe, (and don't quit) nothing is impossible to you." Matthew 17:20

Week 6

"You don't manage people, you correct their behavior and inspire their performance."

"A leader who does not correct people is squandering a precious resource. I think one of the things leaders forget is that people look to us to tell them the truth in terms of how they are doing."

Charles Wang

People do not want to be managed, but they do want you to help them perform their job better. There are at least three ways you can help them improve their performance:

First, help them set ambitious yet realistic goals. Second, be a constant source of encouragement. Be a "Hope Dealer" and their biggest cheerleader. No one ever overdosed on encouragement. Third, constantly communicate the agreed upon expectations; before, during and after their performance.

Consequences are a fact. Each decision and action come with its own consequences, positive or negative. If there is no consequence for poor behavior expect no change or improvement. Great leadership is about knowing how and when to issue the consequence. Does it require major surgery, or just a band-aid?

If there is no reward for outstanding performance, you can expect productivity to slow back down to average. Everyone must be held accountable for his or her performance. Great leaders teach people how to hold themselves accountable and reward them appropriately.

Custom Research, a marketing company with 100 employees, exemplified the appropriate use of consequences. The owners, Jeff and Judy Pope, took a large chunk of their profits to reward the entire staff when they won the coveted Baldridge Award in 1996.

They took everyone to London for five days all expenses paid. Some may say it was extravagant and overkill for a small company. Jeff Pope said, "Not at all, it was money well spent, if you share the pie it gets larger."

Great leaders are forgiving of honest mistakes made in the pursuit of above average performance goals. A bad performance does not make you a bad person. If you want a person's performance to improve support them as a person and help them correct their own actions, never reverse the process.

The excessive use of "sticks and carrots" to correct behavior and increase performance is an overused tool of poor leaders.

Great leaders reach the hearts and minds before they ask for the production of the hands and feet. As a result, they get above average performance without having to use a lot of sticks or carrots. You can manage hands and feet, but never hearts and minds.

"He who heeds discipline shows the way of life, but whoever ignores correction leads others astray." Proverbs 12:1

"Are you a team player, or a solo performer?"

Individual team members normally focus on their own strengths, abilities and how they believe success should look. Most of the time this leads to everyone pulled in a different direction.

Great leaders know it is their task to inspire individual team members to check their ego at the door, set aside personal agendas and cultivate a passion for team solutions and team wins over personal ambition.

After World War II, Chester Nimitz, chief of Naval Operations, wanted to keep alive public interest in naval aviation by forming the Blue Angels Navy Flight Demonstration Squadron. To this day, the Blue Angels' objective and goals are still very clear:

- They select only qualified candidates who consistently operate at peak performance.

- After careful screening, a pilot must receive 16 votes from existing members. If one pilot votes no, the candidate is eliminated.

No questions or explanations are required—that's the level of trust and respect the members have for each other's judgment.

As a Blue Angel, your teammates become your life. Making the squad isn't a one-shot deal either. You are responsible for playing your part by demonstrating value and pursuing excellence on a daily basis. You have to earn the right to wear the crest. Nothing short of total commitment is accepted.

So, would you qualify today to be a Blue Angel? Are you a solo performer, or a team player? Are you prepared, loyal and reliable? When the chips are down can others count on you to sacrifice your own interests ahead of the others?

My definition of great teamwork: "The visible illustration of people who are united with the same purpose." Great leaders know that eighty percent of their time is spent clarifying their organization's purpose and building a team to pursue it with excellence.

Great organizations are constantly building and fine-tuning a culture of unselfish teamwork, people passionate about working together for the same cause. A great culture trumps a great strategy every time. No one has ever climbed Mt Everest alone.

What team member have you "picked up" lately?

"Two are better than one, because they have a good return for their labor: If either of them falls down, one can help the other up. But pity anyone who falls and has no one to help them up" Ecclesiastes 4:9-10

"Why not your best?"

A few years ago, on the TV program, Jeopardy, the final question was, "How many steps does the guard take during his walk across the Tomb of the Unknown Soldier?"

All three contestants missed it. The correct answer is 21 alluding to the 21-gun salute the highest honor given any military or foreign dignitary.

Those who guard the memorial to the unknown fallen heroes make the following commitments:

- Live 2 years in a barracks beneath the tomb.
- Cannot drink alcohol on or off duty for the rest of their lives.
- Cannot swear in public for the rest of their lives.
- Cannot disgrace the uniform in any way.

After their two-year commitment is up, they are given a wreath to wear signifying they served at the tomb. Presently less than 700 are worn. The guards must obey these rules for the rest of their lives or surrender the wreath.

Webster's Dictionary describes "Best" as, "The most excellent, surpassing all others in the most excellent manner in the most suitable way."

The word best occurs 25 times in scripture. In Genesis, Pharaoh told Joseph to give his family the best land in Egypt. The Father in Luke 15 told his servants to give his Prodigal son the best robe. The Apostle Paul in 1 Corinthians 13 said, "Covet earnestly the best gifts."

Great leaders, regardless of the opportunity, give their very best in three ways:

First, they give their best energies to their most important relationships; their God, their family (natural and spiritual) and their marketplace ministry.

Second, they give their best resources to their highest priorities; their "seed," (tithes and offerings) to expand God's Kingdom on earth. Their savings investment in their family's future and stewarding all other resources wisely in living life to its fullest.

Third, they give their best attitudes to their deepest disappointments. They develop a Spirit of Love for those who would harm them. A Spirit of Faith for unanswered prayer, and a Spirit of Hope for the best days that are yet to come.

God gave you his very best in giving his only Son, Jesus. Jesus gave us his very best from making furniture in his dad's carpenter shop to dying on the cross in our place.

If you are not giving your very best to every task, every day—why not?

"You should manage by the book, but you must lead from the heart."

"Being in authority is like being a lady. If you have to remind people you are, you probably aren't"
Margaret Thatcher, Prime Minister, Great Britain

Google assigned their HR Department to identify and rate the attributes of their best and most respected leaders. Surprised to find that technical knowledge ranked last. Instead, listening well and allowing team members make the "big decisions" attracted and kept the best people.

Times of crisis and overwhelming challenges does not require a genius or expert, but managers with average skills and experience to manage by the book and great leaders who provide leadership from the heart. Organizations die every day because those responsible for its survival confuse the two.

Great leadership is making fewer decisions without losing or compromising your influence. It's also retiring your "expert" management skills and asking more and better questions. Stated opinions will never test the wisdom and logic of an idea like well-thought-out questions.

Asking questions always generates better discussions in identifying problems and solutions than making statements. Negotiations always begin after the first statement is made in any conversation.

Great leaders never hesitate to set the course in what seems to be an unsolvable disagreement, but only as a last resort. The best decisions are made after getting the input of the brightest minds closest to the challenge and most effected by the decision.

Shared leadership always produces better decisions and a stronger bond on the leadership team. Gifted people want opportunities to lead and not be managed by being told what to do. They want to accept the challenge and figure out the solution. When you do otherwise you hinder their development and stifle their creativity at best, or worse, you watch them walk away in search of another leader to follow.

You want your managers following the manual in solving today's challenges. However, you want your leadership team to ask more and better questions. The first makes sure all the bases are covered and today's goals are met. The second insures better decisions are made and a compelling future is guaranteed.

Your bottom line, results, will always exceed your greatest expectations when you manage the details by the book, regardless of organization, and you provide leadership from the heart for which this is no manual.

If you must constantly remind people, you're the leader, maybe you aren't. If you are lost in the weeds managing everyday details, I can assure you someone else is leading from their heart, not yours.

"What do you do with problem team members? Ignore them, develop them, or release them?"

When Phil Jackson, NBA title-winning coach of the Chicago Bulls, talks about how he handled Dennis Rodman, the rule-breaking out of control player of the 90s, he said he managed to gain control by giving it up, at least in the mind of Rodman.

Jackson explained, "When we try to control the actions of independent-minded, highly paid talents, it's like putting cattle in a small pasture, they keep breaking through the fence."

Every organization has "A" players, performance and attitude are outstanding. "B" players, performance is average-to-good, and "C" players, performance is barely acceptable to, this person has to go. Poor leaders cater to the "A's," they load up the "B's" with all the work the "C's" should be doing and tolerate the "C's" until they can find a legal reason to fire them.

Great leaders empower and release the "A's," nurture the "B's," and find creative ways to move the "C's" up a level, if possible, before releasing them. They know the cost of replacing a problem team member may cost more than devising a plan to improve their performance.

Before replacing "people with problems" make sure you have made a reasonable investment in making them a viable team member, especially if you invested heavily in the potential you saw when you asked them to join your team. Remember, be slow to appoint to avoid having to disappoint.

Poor leaders try motivating problem people, most of the time without any sustainable success. Our English word, "motivation" comes from two Latin words, meaning, "to come from behind and push." It's difficult motivating anyone to do anything for very long who has no inner desire to improve.

Motivation is a personal decision that only an individual can make, based on their own internal "motivators." There are about as many motivators as there are people so don't spend a lot of time figuring it out. Great leaders inspire properly motivated team members. They deal with motivation first and production expectations second.

Some keys to working with poorly motivated people are; pay attention early and often, identify and address any work-life balance issues, and do they understand their assignment and expectations? Finally, is your leadership the problem?

Most people aren't bad people by nature, they just have a key that you have either overlooked, ignored, or refused to develop. When Dennis Rodman, known as "bad-boy," joined Michael Jordan, a consummate professional, he performed admirably. As a result, the team won six NBA championships.

What about your "problem people?" Did they have those problems when you asked them to join your team, or did they develop them under your leadership? Either way, as a leader you now own the problem and the rest of the team expects you to fix it.

"Vision: is it received, developed, or discovered?"

Father Theodore Hesburgh, former president of Notre Dame University said, "Vision is the essence of leadership."

Visionary leadership is knowing where you want to go, how to get there, and the three things required to make it happen: First, having a clear and compelling vision. Second, articulating and modeling it well. Third, getting your team focused and excited about pursuing it.

Above all, you must be confident and consistent, no one follows an uncertain or faint trumpet. Great leaders develop a clear and compelling vision by using one of the following three approaches. You can impose it, buy it, or forge it through persuasive consensus.

One, imposing a vision can be either by demand or persuasion. Teledyne founder, Henry Singleton, believes an organization is built around a mind with an idea that is aware of the key issues of his generation.

Great leaders stay ahead of the curve and lead from the future, not to the future. They are seasoned visionaries, sharpened by their image of the future. Their ability to empower and connect their teams' everyday efforts to the vision is without question. They guide their organization with confidence and humility, not as overbearing power brokers.

Poor leaders impose their vision through demands often disguised as motivation, but in reality, is manipulation. Great leaders' caste their vision until it becomes the common vision of the team through communication that is vivid and compelling.

Second, you can buy a vision. Consultants will happily create a fashionable mission statement that creates a lot of energy, but few sustainable results. The problem with these "off-the-rack" solutions is they are so generic that they are usually worthless.

Visions can't be bought like a McDonald's burger or Starbucks latte. They can't be a Burger King vision where everyone has it their way. Your team and stakeholders know immediately that you're trying to sell them a second-hand, cut-and-paste dream that they reject immediately.

If they don't, they, are naive and of no real value, you need to release them.

Third, forging a vision. This happens through leadership consensus by encouraging broad contributions in putting flesh on the skeleton you provide. This produces a vision that's the most enduring and effective for long term sustainable results.

At the end of the process you want a vision that is not only compelling but energizes great buy-in by the core leaders and all the stakeholders. You don't forge a vision overnight, but through patience, perseverance, and passion.

If you can't get your team's energized buy-in to the vision, ask yourself the following questions. How passionate am I about it? How often do I show it to them, not just in locker room pep talks, but through my daily actions? How much did I ask the team to contribute in the process?

Week 12

> "Good Leadership is planning for as far as you can see. Great leadership is preparing for what you cannot see."

Great leadership is looking beyond today's horizon and seeing around corners. It is seeing what poor leaders do not see, or they see it and don't know what to do about it.

Great leaders develop their leadership team and plan their strategy for "that" world, the one no one else sees, not the one on today's radar, the one even a poor leader can see.

Why are great leaders able to lead people to places they have never been, and accomplish what others only dream of, but never seem able to accomplish?

Here are seven ways you can be the leader you have always dreamed of and every organization so desperately needs:

1. Believe, speak, and act as if your vision is tomorrow's reality. If you cannot do this, the rest of this list does not matter.

2. Open the eyes of your team to what could be, not just today's reality. Inspire their spirits to believe it will happen, not just could happen.

3. Model daily acts of service that build trust and relational equity with your team and all your stakeholders. Without doing this, you become a drum no one hears.

4. Do not cave in to your critics, or puffed up by your flatterers, or moved by the winds of resistance. Leadership is not for the weak or the arrogant.

5. Stay encouraged while everyone around you may be discouraged. You can never help others be what you are not. Be a hope-dealer, not a dream-killer.

6. Never quit until the goal is reached. Always have the next goal in line before completing your current goal. If you do not, energy wains and momentum is lost.

7. See the leadership potential in everyone and find a way to exploit it, even if it is only leading themselves better. Do not recruit helpers, empower future leaders.

Great leaders focus on tomorrow while average leaders focus on today. Great leaders plan while average leaders think. Great leaders prepare while average leaders plan. Great leaders execute while average leaders prepare. Great leaders win while average leaders watch the clock run out.

Great leaders inspire their team to execute today's plan based on yesterday's preparation. They plan for as far as they can see and remain in a constant mode of preparation for what they cannot see.

What is on your leadership radar today? Do you have a well-thought-out action plan already in place? Is your team prepared and ready to respond?

Until you know the difference between planning for today and preparing for tomorrow your team is going to struggle with your leadership.

Week 13

"Great leaders appreciate value in everyone."

Fritz Kreisler, the world-famous violinist, earned a fortune with his concerts and compositions, but he generously gave most of it away. So, when he discovered an exquisite violin on one of his trips, he was not able to buy it. Later, having raised enough money to meet the asking price, he returned to the seller, hoping to purchase that beautiful instrument. But to his great dismay, it had been sold to a collector.

Kreisler made his way to the new owner's home and offered to buy the violin. The collector said it had become his prized possession, and he would not sell it. Keenly disappointed, Kreisler was about to leave when he had an idea. "Could I play the instrument once more before it is consigned to silence?" He asked.

Permission was granted, and the great virtuoso filled the room with such heart-moving music that the collector's emotions were deeply stirred. "I have no right to keep that to myself," he exclaimed. "It's yours, Mr. Kreisler. Take it into the world, and let people hear it."

To recognize someone is to acknowledge their existence. To appreciate someone is to attach value to their existence. Not everyone has a desire to be recognized publicly, but everyone has a deep need to be appreciated for who they are, not just recognized for what they do.

There are many ways to express appreciation to those who serve on your team. Here are three ways that I have used that might work for you:

First, make every day conversations intentional. No one should think they are indispensable, but neither should they show up every day and feel like they could be replaced at any moment. The way you communicate on a daily basis should make people "feel" they are valued and irreplaceable.

Second, show them how important they are not only to you, but to everyone else on the team. They expect feedback from you, but when it comes from others, it always packs a little more punch. Show your team that they are not only appreciated by you as their leader, but also by their co-workers, those being served, and even by the senior leaders.

Third, challenge them often. Every job comes with less-than-glamorous responsibilities, grunt work. When you only dole out repetitive tasks or tasks below their skill level, you convey that you really do not need their specific, individual talents. But, when you give them a challenging task, you are saying, "I know you're capable of this and I trust you to do a great job."

As was the case with Fritz Kreisler, who on your team, if truly appreciated, could provide value far beyond what you believe is possible or expect?

Unexpressed appreciation has little, if any, value. Great mechanics know that machines work better with a little attention. Great leaders know that people perform better with a little appreciation.

Week 14

"Can you hand me a can of tomato soup?"

I remember a story about a little girl who was afraid of the dark. She lived in an old farmhouse where they kept food in a pantry that to her was dark and intimidating. Her mother, preparing dinner, asks her to get a can of tomato soup out of the pantry. She peered behind the curtain leading to the pantry that had no light or windows, being scared she ran back to her mother empty-handed.

"Where's the soup?" asked her mother. The little girl, shaking, replied, "Its dark in there, I'm afraid." Three times her mother sent her back, and each time she went as far as the curtain and ran back without the soup.

Finally, her mother said, "Don't be afraid of the dark, Jesus is in the dark, he'll protect you." Slowly the little girl returned to the pantry curtain, pulled it back and fearfully said, "Jesus, if you're in there would you please hand me a can of tomato soup?"

It's a funny story and while most people outgrow their fear of the dark as a child, most adults still lack the courage to face the unknown or uncertainty. Jack Welch, one of the 20th Century's top corporate leaders as CEO of General Electric, spent most of his time developing leaders.

Jack constantly drilled the potential senior leaders and managers on what separates great leaders from the average is the "courage" to make the tough calls decisively, with fairness and absolute integrity, especially "in the dark" and when the outcome is uncertain.

Courage will permeate and transform everything you do. It's the crucial seasoning in the leadership skill mix God has blessed you with. Take away courage from a leader and you are left with a functionary manager who can only enforce the manual.

Rules and regulations are needed to keep order. However, they are not the tools of leaders who create the future, they are the tactics of managers who only respond to today's challenges. There are no manuals for the future. You need guts to enforce the rulebook, but you need courage to create the future and they are not the same.

Someone once said, "Courage is fear that has said its prayers." People are inspired by leaders who are brutally honest about the risks and obstacles but go for it anyway. Adversity energizes and motivates courageous leaders, but it quickly quenches the fire in leaders who lack courage.

There is a fine line between faith and fanaticism and only courageous leaders walk that line. Weak leaders follow in the shadows, a much safer place. When hitting short-term difficulties, remember, it is your long-term goals that create the courage to go on. Seldom does life "hand you the tomato soup." You must go into the unknown and get it. That takes courage.

"If you falter in times of trouble, how small is your strength." Proverbs 24:10

"A 15-minute vision checkup."

Ask your core leaders these seven questions. If they answer no or show hesitation you are overdue for a vision checkup.

If your core leaders show any doubt rest assured the team members on the outer edge do not have a clue. It is the "outer-edge" team members that have the initial and most frequent contact with those you serve or are trying to reach.

1. IMAGINABLE: Does our vision convey a compelling picture of our future?

2. DESIRABLE: Does our vision appeal and grab the attention of at least two generations?

3. FEASIBLE: Is our vision built on reasonable, stretchable and achievable goals?

4. FOCUSED: Does our vision guide and dominate our decision-making process?

5. FLEXIBLE: Does our vision allow for individual creativity and changing conditions?

6. COMMUNICABLE: Can all our core leaders "Tell our story" and describe our vision in 100 words or less?

7. EXECUTABLE: Is our strategy (action plan) well-conceived, understood and embraced by all team members?

You get the best results when your team members feel they can be brutally honest, especially with their leader. Great leaders keep drilling down until they discover what every team member really thinks, not just what they think the leader wants to hear.

Until you have that degree of openness and honesty by everyone on the team you have not taped into the full potential of your team. Until you ask your team for just a little more than they think they can give, you won't get all they can give. That takes commitment, trust and honest answers to these seven questions.

When is the last time you and your team had a vision checkup? Poor attitudes, low energy and lack of engagement may indicate its time.

"Positive leadership influence. How you get it, use it, and lose it."

Building relational equity is the key to gaining positive influence with those you lead. Trust is the driver of all relationships. Without trust, people may comply but only until they find a way out. Without trust few people will adopt your values, pursue the vision in any meaningful way, and stay with you for the long haul.

Managers are rewarded for reducing costs and reaching goals. However, with leaders it's about developing people and increasing team effectiveness. Managers put people on the cost side of the ledger while leaders view them as assets. Managers value people for what they do. Leaders value people for who they are. While both are vital who do you think has the most influence?

Above average leadership influence begins with creating a culture of continuous improvement in three ways:

First, everyone must love change and improvement as a way of life. Second, everyone must buy-in to small improvements that when compounded, create big wins. Third, everyone must have confidence in their leader and fellow team members that creates uncommon synergy for change and improvement.

People decide what they think about you before they decide what they think about your leadership. Great leaders know you must gain leadership influence before you can use it effectively. Poor leaders constantly use their positional authority because they fail in gaining positive influence and become impatient.

You get the most influence and you get it quicker by connecting with the hearts and minds of your team members before asking for the efforts of their hands and feet. There is a political and emotional component to every relationship. How do I feel and is my influence gaining or losing?

Never forget the critical balance between competence and warmth when pursuing leadership influence. If you do, you have to rely on your power and authority to push people to produce because your ability to influence them in a positive way is gone.

Week 17

"Never overestimate your personal value or leadership shelf life."

According to Yale University's management psychologist, Dr. Clayton Alderfer, "Genuine leaders rarely radiate I-am-the-greatest tone." All great leaders have a healthy mix of confidence and humility.

Leaders who refer to "my" business, "my" organization, or "my" church as a personal possession, usually have an ego that cannot be confined in a football stadium. Any successful effort is built through the collective effort of many dedicated team members, Leadership 101.

Ego versus humility is a critical balancing act. Without an ego very little of significant value happens. However, an inflated or out-of-bounds ego leaves a lot of blood on the trail in the drive to success.

Naive leaders who think they are indispensable, even for a day a week much less an extended vacation hardly understand their place in the grand scheme of life and are totally out of touch about understanding the shelf life of their leadership effectiveness.

Many myopic leaders are manipulated or dethroned by money, flattery, selfish glory, or "they can't do it without me" syndrome.

Although many leaders are victims of their own runaway egos, other leaders must guard against an equally dangerous pitfall, excessive modesty or false humility. Excessive modesty is usually a sincere, but a misguided self-depreciation of the value God placed in everyone to whom He gave life. False humility is an attempt to deceive others by projecting someone you are not. Neither serve leaders well.

The Apostle Paul in Romans 12:3 said, "Don't think more of yourself than you ought." When you look in the mirror be brutally about your personal abilities and accomplishments but not to the point of personal injury.

God only made one of you, celebrate "who" you are, not just what you do. Others will celebrate what you do but seldom who you are. Learn to cheer for yourself once in a while just don't inflate your value or extend your leadership shelf life beyond its expiration date.

"Leadership excellence, is it a goal or way of life?"

Bill Bradley, former three-time U.S. Senator from NJ, Rhodes Scholar at Oxford, and all-American basketball player at Princeton, attended a summer basketball camp at age 15. While there, basketball great "Easy" McCauley told him, "If you're not getting the most out of your ability during practice, there'll be someone out there one day working the most of his ability and when you play against him, he'll have the advantage."

Neither critics nor competitors should determine your level of excellence. What is the difference between success and excellence? You measure success by comparing yourself with others. You determine excellence by your efforts versus your potential.

Others reward your success and it comes to only a few, but excellence is available to everyone if they make it a way of life and not an occasional goal. A person with a spirit of excellence never looks at the task and then decides if it is worthy of excellence.

Studies have shown that to achieve excellence in anything commonly requires approximately 10,000 hours of dedicated practice over ten years. The word 'arête' is French, meaning, "having the edge." The ancient Greeks used it to describe the act of living up to your potential.

Mark 7:37 says, "He (Jesus) has done all things well." The context of this verse refers to his healing ministry. However, I believe it described everything he did. I believe he worked in his Father's carpenter shop with the same spirit of excellence.

Great leaders know it is not the greatness of the task that makes a leader stand out, but it's doing every task with greatness that separates the great leaders from the good and average.

What average task will you do this week with greatness? What person who feels average will feel great because of their association with you? My friend, that is what real leadership is all about.

Week 19

"Are you an asset or liability?"

When you walk into the lobby of the ServiceMaster headquarters building in Downers Grove, Illinois, you see on your right a curving marble wall that stretches ninety feet and stands eighteen feet tall. Carved prominently in that stonewall in letters four feet high are their four corporate values:

* To honor God in all we do

* To help people develop

* To pursue excellence

* To grow profitably

Is it any wonder then that return on equity has averaged 50 percent and stock values have grown in value from one dollar per share to over fifty-four dollars per share? That kind of sustained performance does not happen unless God and people are assets to be esteemed and not "tools" to be used for turning a profit or personal ambition.

In today's America God and people are quickly becoming liabilities and no longer assets. When ServiceMaster first established their corporate values and made them prominent, it raised eyebrows. The critics asked, "Aren't you on shaky ground when you try to mix God and profits? And what about employees who do not choose to behave the way you do, aren't you forcing your religious beliefs on them?"

We live and work in a pluralistic society where many question the very existence of God and our right as believers to represent Him in the marketplace. When determining whether you are an asset, or a liability keep in context which Kingdom comes first the secular kingdoms of this earth or the Kingdom of Light. One is temporal, the other is eternal. I believe you must be an asset to both but for different reasons.

In your drive to be an asset in today's marketplace, which gives you the platform to represent the Kingdom of Light, do not allow your work environment to be emasculated to a neutrality of no belief at best, or worse, one of disbelief. You are an asset to your workplace when you add to the bottom-line profits. You are an asset to the Kingdom of Light when you live your faith without apology in a way that honors God and adds value and dignity to your team members.

"For even I (Jesus) came to earth not to be served but to serve others and give his life as a ransom for many" Mark 10:45.

Anyone with a servant's heart is an asset to any company and certainly to God's kingdom. Christians do a lot of damage when they try to be an asset in God's kingdom but are a liability to the company in which they represent Him. And vice-versa, they work hard being an asset to the company but fail as an ambassador for God's kingdom.

Week 20

"Energizing your team for change is your greatest leadership challenge."

Astronaut James Irwin said, "You think going to the moon was the most scientific project ever, but they literally threw us in the direction of the moon. We had to adjust course every ten minutes and landed only 50 feet inside a 500-mile radius of our target."

On that mission every change, no matter how small, was essential to success. So, it is with yours. If you resist even the slightest change long enough, you may find yourself off course, too late to adjust, and must abort the mission.

What causes a lack of behavioral or organizational change? Team members are seldom the problem but get most of the blame. Senior leaders create most of their own problems by their lack of leadership in one or more of the following four areas:

First, lack of clarity about the rationale not only for the daily action plan, but more so for the long-term goals and strategy for change. People seldom buy into what they cannot see and understand.

Second, lack of commitment and passion for change by the core leadership team. Passion, or the lack of it, is contagious. There must be consensus and one hundred percent buy in by the core team. If not, delay the change or change players on the team.

Third, lack of accountability on a regular basis to reinforce positive sustainable change. Without accountability there is no improvement of what already exists much less changing it.

Fourth, lack of trust by the team in their Leaders' decision-making skill in leading change. Trust is the glue that holds teams together when they face the unknown and the lubricant that enables them to flow together till the needed change becomes a way of life.

Average leaders can keep the car between the guardrails most of the time. However, it takes outstanding leaders to lead when the way forward is no longer on the map and current conditions demand a change of direction.

"Those who cannot change their minds cannot change anything." George Bernard Shaw

Why not ask your leadership team which of the four areas above challenge them the most? Great leaders constantly ask this question and many others that make their leadership vulnerable and open for inspection. Weak leaders avoid questions about their leadership at all costs.

Technology-driven smart phones, tablets and laptops, microwave ovens, computer-flown airplanes, robots that can do just about anything, most kid toys and big box stores filled gadgets unheard-of a generation ago.

They are today's reality as a result of that first trip to the moon led by men and women not threatened by change. The wealthiest corporations on earth today were founded and continue to be led by leaders who declare war on the status quo every day.

Remember, without change your organization has no future. Without you personally changing your team remains stuck in "today" and only dreams about a better tomorrow.

"BUSY BUT NOT PRODUCTIVE"

"The least productive people are usually the ones who are most in favor of holding meetings." Thomas Sowell

Great leaders constantly monitor their core values, core strengths and critical resources. All three are vital. They make sure they line up and create forward momentum every day.

Doing many things' means you are busy. Doing the right things on a timely basis means you are productive and create measurable value. This is what creates long-term employment and personal satisfaction.

Here are five signs you are busy but probably not productive:

First, attending too many non-productive meetings. Most meetings are poorly planned, over-managed and usually cost more than they are worth.

Second, doing other people's work instead of your own. Non-producers are always looking for someone else to cover for their own lack of effort.

Third, living for the daily "fire drill," doing the urgent and ignoring the important. Top producers do the important when it's seldom urgent. Nonproductive people are always busy, seem to live in a constant state of urgency and accomplish little.

Fourth, majoring on the trivial in order to avoid doing the uncomfortable. Great leaders make a living doing what poor leaders find uncomfortable and find every excuse to avoid.

Fifth, you are constantly stuck in "social media" and information overload. You do not have to respond to every email, Twitter, Facebook, LinkedIn and Instagram to name a few.

There is an alternative to busyness. It is called creating a reality beyond the urgent. If you desire focused productivity over busyness and urgency, ask yourself the following four questions:

What do I really want in my limited time on earth? What am I doing today that supports my deepest passions? If I knew the number of my days, what would I stop doing and start doing? Am I spending more time with people who celebrate me or tolerate me? Before you create your daily "To Do" list, answer these four questions.

It is very difficult to measure busyness—activity without results. Productivity is the result of focused efforts with measurable goals. Is it valuable and worth doing if it cannot be measured? Compensation and reward should be given based on measurable results not how hard you work.

"The man on the top of the mountain didn't fall there." Vince Lombardi

Many are busy and working hard going around the mountain but forget the goal is to make it to the top!

"Great leaders do three things for their team."

The Bible is the greatest leadership manual ever written. Corporations, organizations and churches that are the most profitable, effective and sustainable use biblical principles whether they understand them, agree with or promote them.

There is a story in Joshua 1:9-15 that illustrates this truth. Here are three leadership principles found in that text:

First, "Be strong and courageous" (v.9). Your leadership significance expands or shrinks in proportion to the risk. Strength and courage are not demonstrated through great speeches but through predetermined actions. You can follow from a distance, but you cannot lead from there.

Second, "Crossover ahead of your brothers" (v.14). Leaders are always ahead in pursuing the vision because they are the most passionate about winning. They don't possess the mission; the mission possesses them. They teach their team the importance of expectation management and how to lead to the future—not just win today.

Third, "Help your brothers" (v.14). How long do great leaders invest in their team? Until they "possess the land," reach the goal! The race is not finished until every team member crosses the finish line. Team success should never cause personal discouragement or failure of any individual team member.

When you do what you are called to do, the reason you are called "Leader," your team will respond as did Joshua's in Verse 16: "And they answered Joshua, we will do whatever you command us, and we will go wherever you send us."

Success through teamwork does not just happen. As the leader, you must make clear and compelling strategic plans and focus everyone's individual effort on the team's goal. Relational skills and a spirit of teamwork must have value above technical skill and position all the time.

There are no limits for any team when they are led by a leader who puts these three principles ahead of his own ambition and personal comfort.

Week 23

"Every management problem you have today was a leadership failure yesterday."

Leaders who do not understand their role as a strategic leader will constantly try to overcome their leadership failures with better management solutions. They remain mired in their day-to-day management problems and not address their leadership failures that could have prevented most of them.

Whatever shows up on their daily radar screen is where they focus all their time and energy. There never seems to be anything left in the tank with which to focus their leadership strengths on the future and a plan to prevent possible problems is non-existent.

The word strategic by definition means: [Relating to the identification of long-term or overall aims and interests and the means of achieving them]

If you have strategic (future) leadership responsibilities your primary function is modeling and communicating—not managing the mission, vision and core values. If you do not, who will? Your secondary role is developing, empowering and inspiring your team to win in the future—not just solve today's problems.

You can either manage your organization or you can lead it. You cannot do both at the same time and do both well. If you try you will do neither well. You will end up frustrating both those you lead and those you are trying to serve.

Are you leading, creating the future? Or managing, responding to the next urgency or crisis? A quick look at your calendar, your "To Do List" and your appointment schedule will quickly tell you.

If you're the one responsible for the creating the future and you spend more than twenty percent of your time on current problems chances are you are managing the present, not leading to the future. If you want to reduce your management problems quit trying to be a better manager and develop better leadership skills.

You create a better today with effective and efficient management solutions. That's why you have "managers." However, you only create a better tomorrow through strategic planning and rigorous execution. That's why you're called a leader.

"But have you not heard? I decided this long ago. Long ago I planned it, and now I am making it happen."

Isaiah 37:26 (NLT)

The BP deep-well oil rig crisis in the Gulf of Mexico a few years ago was first a failure of BP leadership before it ever became a management problem that couldn't be overcome, even by their best managers.

What is your priority today, leading or managing? Not sure, look at your task list for today!

Week 24

"Great leaders earn respect. Poor leaders demand compliance."

You can demand compliance from those on your team but only from those who are fearful or lack confidence. However, the fearful or those lacking confidence will many times let you down when you need them the most.

Sometimes even those who respect you and your leadership are not always the easiest to lead but you can count on them when the chips are down, and tough decisions must be made.

How do you earn that respect?

1. Get to know your team by constantly building relational equity. You can never have too many deposits in their emotional bank accounts.
2. Gaining respect involves being competent in what your leadership position requires, modeling servant-leadership and keeping your word.
3. Create a zone of separation where your team cannot come. In that zone, you create things for them they cannot provide for themselves. Without that zone, familiarity sets in and respect fades.
4. Respect for your leadership begins and develops on the front lines where your team members live, not watching power points and listening to pep talks in meetings you control.
5. Future leaders learn respect by watching "adults," not people in positions of power or authority displaying emotional immaturity and childish behavior.

Without respect, you may be their boss, but you will never be their leader. Respect and compliance are both given. Which does your leadership deserve?

> "Great leaders live for their team. Good leaders invest in their team. Poor leaders use their team for their own benefit."

Someone conducted a survey among people who lived to be over 100. Most people would expect the cause was eating healthy food, miracle drugs and strenuous exercise. Some of those reasons contributed to their longevity, but the one thing these centenarians had in common was-- they had a purpose beyond themselves.

Do you have a cause that compels you to get out of bed every morning, or do you awake every day without a passion for something outside your own interest? Living for a cause greater than yourself means refusing to live trapped in fear or the very limited dimensions of a self-centered world.

Too many people are like the man who said, "No matter what I'm working on, I'd rather be doing something else." Regardless of age or circumstances, everyone needs a cause great enough to focus your energies and strong enough to energize you on your worst day.

Just as God made Goliath for David's benefit and development, God has a cause made especially for you. A challenge that needs confronting or a situation that needs changing.

The giant that caused the officers of Israel's army to tremble in fear, and King Saul to cower in the palace, was the challenge that launched David's rise to be the greatest King of his day.

At age twelve, Jesus said, "I must be about my Father's business." Twenty-one years later while dying for the sins of all mankind on the cross He cried out, "It is finished." These two statements framed His life on earth. The greatest leader who ever lived, lived for a cause greater than Himself.

Until you find the cause for which you were born you are not ready to lead. Until you understand that great leadership is about using your abilities and influence for the benefit of others, at best you can only make periodic investments in others.

You exist for the team, they do not exist for you. The sooner you learn that, the sooner great people will stand in line to be on your team and follow your leadership.

"Believe, when you are most unhappy, that there is something you can do in the world. So long as you can sweeten another's pain, life is not in vain."

Helen Keller

"Before you release the 'vision-drainers' on your team try the following…"

First, describe what you have observed as negative in their behavior. Be fair and honest without being judgmental. Discuss with them what needs to improve and why.

If they agree and show a willingness to improve move to step two. If they do not, help them find a place where their abilities and attitude are a better fit.

Second, be clear about what is acceptable behavior and performance. Provide additional teaching and training if necessary. Remember, no amount of teaching or training can make up for a poor attitude or non-productive behavior.

Trying to lead or coach vision-drainers is frustrating at best and a team-spirit killer if allowed to continue for very long. The longer you allow vision-drainers to remain, the more frustrated your vision-makers become and the sooner they leave.

Third, make sure they understand the consequences of continued poor performance and set a deadline for improvement. Have them summarize your conversation and commit to making the needed changes.

Winning or losing is first an attitude before it's an action or an outcome. No one is blessed with all Vision-Makers, not even Jesus. However, he did turn a lot of losers into winners because of his attitude toward them and his willingness to not give up on anyone making a sincere effort.

Before you release any team member make sure it's because of their attitude and lack of effort, not because of your frustration, lack of teaching and training or unwillingness to go the second-mile.

Most of the time you have to move tons of dirt to find an ounce of gold. If you thought they were worth asking to join your team originally, do not get weary in moving the dirt till you find their value.

It takes a great leader to find the gold, especially when it is hidden deep. As a sophomore, Michael Jordan was cut from his high-school basketball team. However, he went on to become one of the greatest NBA players of all time.

No one starts out as "great." They must believe God put greatness in them and then find a leader who's willing to help them move a lot of dirt to find it!

"If it's all about you, your leadership is not only unhealthy, it dies with you."

"It's All About Me" became a top-ten hit on Billboard's Hot 100 the week of May 16, 1998. It fared better on the R&B Singles Chart, reaching number two.

I met a leader several years ago who said, "I've been in the limelight so long, I'm getting sunburned." I thought, how emotionally immature can a leader be and how tragic for those following him. Sorry to say, but that song and the irresponsible statement of a so-called leader sum up too much of today's leadership.

Unselfish leadership, regardless of venue, is rare today. I often say, "Great leadership is like the Abominable Snowman. He's rarely seen, but his footprints are everywhere."

If providing significant and sustainable leadership is your desire, then be "seen" less, say less and move over and use your influence to help others find their way to center stage.

Use these seven actions to demonstrate that you understand your leadership influence and responsibility involves more than your skills, tasks and titles. It's about elevating and empowering others:

1. Get over yourself. Leadership is about leveraging your influence for the sake of others, not for your own self interests.
2. Be easy to understand and follow. Be predictable and avoid surprises. Great leaders make the complex challenges simple and the cloudy things clear.
3. Encourage others to dream and stop flooding every meeting with only your dreams and how much you need your team to help you fulfill them.
4. Lead with informed boldness. Maintain the posture of a warrior, but never be stupid. Bravery means understanding the risks and possessing the courage to attack the challenge in spite of them.

5. Remain focused on the vision. Great leaders constantly move their team toward a preferred and agreed upon future without giving in to distractions.

6. Create and maintain a winning culture, leadership's number one daily priority. Managers study the operations manual and hold people responsible for their actions. Leaders create a winning environment and hold people responsible for their attitude. Great organizations have both.

7. Make informed decisions. Providing accurate, adequate and shared information, coupled with open and honest discussion, is the only way that happens. The more power and authority you have, the fewer decisions you should make. It's called developing and empowering others, "Leadership 101."

Leadership is just as much about helping others achieve their dreams as it is seeing your own come true. "Even the Son of Man came to serve, not be served." (Mark 10:45)

"If your actions inspire others to dream more, learn more, do more and become more--you are a leader."

John Quincy Adams

"Is your leadership creating a culture of justice and fairness, or one of confusion and mistrust?"

"Organizations that are willing to share, withhold in order to further the growth, willing to try to get a better atmosphere through a demonstration of fairness and cooperation, those will win in the end." E.O. Wilson, two-time Pulitzer Prize winner.

Justice means giving and receiving what a person deserves. Whereas, fairness is the ability to make judgments that are concrete and specific to a particular situation. Determining what is just and fair is one of leaderships' greatest challenges on a daily basis.

When growing up if there was only one piece of pie left, Mom let one of us make the cut and the other choose the first piece. Oh, if life were only that simple! Can you be just and not fair? Or, can you be fair and not just?

It is very difficult keeping team members energized and loyal if they feel others are taking advantage, regardless if that person is in the corner office or in the cubicle next door. If people perceive they are being treated unfairly, they will eventually stop performing, start imitating those they perceive are being favored or join another team.

Great leaders operate on principles of fairness because they know it inspires better performance, loyalty and retention. Honesty and integrity are primarily dealing with individuals while justice and fairness is about team dynamics. Work environments without both values are not a fun place to go every day.

Your job as a leader is to change that. If you do not you can expect a lot of unhappy campers and watch productivity drop. You cannot make everyone happy all the time. At some point, those who refuse to be team players must be let go. No matter how much you do for them, in their eyes it is never just or fair.

Leaders who do not lead with a basic sense of justice and fairness, soon lose the trust and loyalty of even their most faithful followers. Great leaders never use their position or influence to make and enforce arbitrary decisions for their own good or personal ambitions, but always do what is best for the team. If you want to retain your best team members, maintaining a work environment of justice and fairness is your best bet!

"Blessed are those who maintain justice, who constantly do what is right."
Psalms 106:3

"Great leaders create margin; good leaders pay on time and poor leaders ask for an extension."

One of the most common challenges in the 21st Century is feeling stressed and chronically overwhelmed. Too many leaders are busy, tired and feel stretched because there always seems to be more to do than we have time or energy to do it.

When life's demands appear to be greater than our resources, the result is stress. We feel stressed about our lack of time, physical and emotional energy, relational demands and financial pressure.

Stress then shows up as irritability, anxiety, not eating well, poor sleep habits, not exercising regularly and making hasty and usually poor decisions. Stress comes to everyone, especially those who try to live and lead without a margin.

The concept of "margin" is based on the premise that it is wise to leave space in our lives to deal with the unexpected or unplanned events that always arise. This is in contrast with our tendency to pack our schedule full, or (as some people frame it) to "make the most of our time."

Change starts with awareness and acceptance of present reality. If we do not think how we are living creates problems for us, our family or our vocation, then we will not change. So, it might be wise to start with being brutally honest with your schedule, finances, tasks and commitments.

Look at your life and see if the occurrence of "unexpected events" are fairly common in your life and create stress because you don't allow space in which to deal with these unplanned events.

Great leadership is not about how hard you work, but how smart you work. If you do not learn to fully disengage, you will never fully engage with passion, energy and effectiveness.

Without margins, interruptions become frustrating roadblocks rather than opportunities to see God. When we operate at or near 100% capacity, we have no time for interruptions.

No opportunities to see God outside of our pre-ordained to-do lists and jam-packed schedules. Yet, I would argue this is primarily where God is found, in the margins and "interruptions" of life.

Leaders who lead without margin not only damage their own life and relationships, they lead organizations into failure every day.

Pause and give thanks today for the good things in your life and put some time in your schedule to do nothing! Many times, doing nothing is the best way to accomplish more.

"How well do you balance your tasks and your relationships?"

If the interaction with your team is focused solely on completing the task, I would argue that you have a functional, but not a personal relationship and certainly not a friendship. Both are critical for providing leadership excellence and sustainable success.

A relationship of convenience or production expectations provides little, if any, relational equity or a healthy work environment. No relational substance below the surface equals no margin for strife or strain that challenge all relationships.

Without relational margin with your team members you are constantly making demands on overdrawn accounts. That may work in the short term, but without eliminating the negative relational balance, your best team members will soon leave you for greener pastures.

Your success as a leader is not so much from your positional authority, but from valuing relationships in a way that your team members know you understand their world and how they feel. That is something that the growing field of technology and absent or remote leadership styles will never replace.

There is a political and emotional component to every relationship and every interaction and decision within that relationship. The political component determines how your influence will increase or decrease. The emotional component determines how you will feel about it.

Leaders who forget these two components struggle to stay above the waterline at best, or worse, drown in failure because they want to lead without significant relationships above them, around them, or below them.

Would your staff say you care more about them as a person or more about what they produce? Not sure? Why not do an anonymous survey and know for certain!

Week 31

"You are a leader—not God"

The pattern is all too familiar. You cheerfully and willingly meet another person's need, then bask in the new attention and admiration. However, praises and admiration soon turn to resentment when a need arises that you cannot fill. It is not long before the disillusioned and disappointed tear down their "failed God."

God warns every leader in Isaiah 42:8, "I am the Lord; that is my name! I will not give my glory to anyone else, nor share my praise with carved idols." (NLT) When you forget you are a reflector and not the source, your ability to significantly influence your team soon ends.

In order to avoid having people look to you to meet their needs rather than God, requires humility and redirection. Jesus said in Matthew 6:14, "But when you give alms, don't let your left hand know what your right hand is doing. Do what you do in secret, so God can reward you openly."

Great leaders graciously accept the admiration and respect of the people they serve. However, they redirect their hearts toward the source of both the love and the ability to serve.

If you do not direct peoples' trust and expectations to a source outside of yourself, you set them up for unfulfilled expectations. Unfulfilled expectations still bring life's greatest disappointments. Never forget, you are not God. You are only a channel.

No leader has arrived at the point of perfection. Every leader is still striving to overcome their own issues. Regardless of talent and ability, no leader is better than anyone else. They are simply appointed, elected or chosen to lead at this point in time.

New leaders must reject the thought that they are not worthy and qualified to serve. If they do not, their team will lack confidence in their leadership.

Long-serving leaders must reject the notion that they are the source of their own success. If they do not, their team will soon see their lack of credibility to lead.

"Don't forget to fill the tanks of your average producers!"

Great leaders resist recognizing only top performers. All great organizations are built on a lot of good middle producers and a few outstanding performers who have learned to deal with their ego in a healthy way.

Every team member not only deserves recognition but requires it. They need it individually and for their efforts as a team player. Most people scramble for it and feel starved without it. Never forget, no one ever overdosed on respect and encouragement.

Recognition and respect are the energy that fuels the human spirit. Great leaders fuel all team members, not just their top performers. Do not wait till they are on empty, top off their tanks every day!

Great leaders use healthy relationships to inspire their team while poor leaders bully people using fear and manipulation. Manipulation is using fear or misguided incentives for producing short-term gains without concern for the long-term problems they create.

Productive individuals and teamwork are the result of great leaders instilling confidence and recognizing their good average producers while allowing them to share in the limelight created by the team's mature superstars.

Great teams have both! Have you identified both on your team? When was the last time you filled up their emotional fuel tanks?

"What motivates people to follow you?"

A compelling vision is like a trailer for a blockbuster movie. A 30-minute clip highlighting the movie that compels you to watch the entire story. Like a movie trailer, the vision keeps you focused on your dream and doing whatever it takes to see it happen.

Many organizational vision statements are like a B-rated movie. The plot is vague, the acting is second-rate, you regret buying the ticket regardless of how cheap and the whole experience drains your energy. Sound familiar?

Only "sick people" sit through a bad movie twice. Yet this describes the daily experience of millions of team members who sit through second-rate leadership visions day after day simply because they need the job. Is your team following you because the vision is compelling, or because you hand them a check every week?

Your vision is a picture of everyone's hoped-for result. What the end looks like, what we produce and how we function every day. Does everyone on your team "see" the same thing, work toward the same goals and operate with the same values?

The vision must not only resonate with you, but with everyone following you. If not, conflict, confusion and unfulfilled dreams are in your future. The vision must reach your team's inner aspirations. The language must translate into a realistic strategy and its fulfillment challenging, but achievable.

If you want an energized team following you, the vision must be clear, compelling and easy to explain. Even if implementing your vision is complicated, explaining it should not be.

Your vision cannot be abstract or vague and compelling at the same time. If you want your team excited about the future, show it to them often until your vision becomes "our vision."

"The greatest achievement was at first and for a time a dream. The oak sleeps in the acorn, the bird waits in the egg, and in the highest vision of the soul, a waking angel stirs. Dreams are the seedlings of realities."

James Allen

What embryonic dream rests in your heart waiting to birth into a compelling vision that causes others to follow for no other reason than seeing the dream become a reality?

People following you only for a check, a perk or a position of influence never help you fulfill your vision—instead they greatly hinder the chance of everyone seeing the team's vision become a reality.

"Is God at the heart of your business plan?"

"For I know the plans I have for you. They are plans for good and not for disaster; to give you a future and a hope."
Jeremiah 29:11

According to Psalms 127:1, if your business or marketplace effort is not built on a foundation of Godly principles, then your labor is truly in vain regardless of how successful you may be in the eyes of man.

All great leaders have a well-thought-out blueprint to guide them on their journey to success. If your plan is the key to your success, then God's Word should be the foundation of your plan.

God has not promised to sustain or prosper any business or marketplace effort that does not reflect His principles. When you obey His commands, principles and plans for your business, He will lead you to unlimited prosperity and sustainable success.

You are more than a business owner or professional, you are an ambassador for God's Kingdom, serving many times in a very hostile environment. An ambassador is generally defined as a diplomatic official of the highest rank. (2 Corinthians 5:20). Your professional success is to be used for His glory, not just your own success.

Your marketplace achievements are to be shining examples for others to witness God's influence in your life and efforts. It is up to you as God's representative to set the standard for everyone else. When you do, you will have to use very few words to proclaim the goodness of God. The marketplace value you create will speak for itself.

If you are struggling in your business or marketplace effort, check your plan. Is there a clear connection between your plan and God's covenant purpose for your life and Kingdom calling?

If not, the sooner you make the needed corrections, the sooner His covenant promises will start showing up on a daily basis. Why should an unbeliever in the same business be more successful?

"And all these blessings shall come upon you and overtake you. Heed the voice of the Lord your God." Deuteronomy 28:2

What is the first adjustment you need to make today to better connect your business or marketplace effort to God's covenant promises?

Week 35

"Does your team know how to create a win?"

Great leaders always define the expectations with any assignment they give to their team. Unfulfilled expectations still bring life's greatest disappointments.

Your ability to attract and retain valuable people increases in direct proportion to your ability to define expectations when they first join your team.

Good people who cannot find fulfillment and value associating with you and your team should not stay around too long. If they do, they damage the team and diminish your leadership in the eyes of the rest of the team.

Refresh, retrain, or remove them--sooner rather than later. Who is your team today that needs inspired? Who needs additional training? Who needs released so that they can find a better fit?

Leaders are disappointed because their team does not fulfill their expectations. Team members are discouraged because their leader never defined and showed them how to win.

Are you sure your team knows what you expect? How do you know? Is it fair to hold people accountable for expectations that have never been defined? If those expectations are not written, do they really exist?

Great leaders recruit the right people, make sure they understand the expectations of their assignment and provide significant opportunities for them to win on a regular basis.

"Core Values, they effect everything"

Upon the death of President Franklin Roosevelt, near the end of World War II, Sam Rayburn, Speaker of the House, took V.P. Harry Truman aside and said, "You're going to have a lot of people around you telling you what a great man you are, Harry. But you and I both know you aren't."

Truman ended up being a pretty good president because his core values were fundamentally strong, and they guided his presidency.

Most organizations talk about core values; why you do and don't do certain things. They reveal what you stand for and determine how you govern your personal life, lead your team and create your workplace environment.

But, if given a blank piece of paper, could your core leadership team write down 5-7 non-negotiable principles that dictate how you live your personal leadership values or create the culture where you lead? How about those at the front door or who answer the phone?

After thirteen years of traveling over 250 days a year and working with hundreds of church and marketplace leaders, the lack of understanding and commitment by their teams to the same core values created most of their leadership and organizational problems.

Most leaders think their organization is values-based. They think everyone knows, supports and lives them every day. This assumption by senior leaders creates most of their time-consuming and energy-draining challenges.

If you do not think core values effect everything, ask your team to list your team's core values by memory. If they cannot, I would bet the farm that most of your leadership and organizational challenges are values-related issues driven by either uninformed or uncaring team members.

Your leadership life will be easier and more fulfilling when you get your "core values statements" out of the file, take the framed plaques off the wall and make them a way of life for everyone!

"Keys to winning on a daily basis"

Great leaders bring a winning attitude and operational value on a daily basis. If you are not consistently winning, (reaching your goals) then you may need to change the way you are organized, change the way you operate, or maybe change who's on your team.

The connection between your team members, your strategy (action plan) and the way you go about your routine tasks must be strong, clear and simple. If any of these are foggy, winning consistently will be a constant challenge.

If you have the right players on your team. If your structure is consistently bringing operational value and everyone knows how they create value and you're still not winning, then take an honest look at your strategy, your action plan for success.

Your strategy must do three key things. First, it must define your goals. Second, it must focus and guide your team's daily efforts. Finally, it must determine your structure and create a simple and clear path to success.

As the leader, you may be able to "connect the dots." However, until your team members can connect them, winning on a regular basis will remain just out of reach and soon de-energize everyone.

Winning every day requires more than just hard work and having the right people on the team. Winning on a daily basis and seeing your vision become a reality is determined by getting those three strategy steps right.

"Commit your work to the Lord and your plans will be established."
Proverbs 16:3

"Invest in your leadership team as people, not as a depreciating asset."

People do not work for organizations. They work for people. Most people do not quit their job, they quit their leader. Just because you give someone a title and call them a leader, does not make it so. Without giving them proper training and support, it will never happen.

Some organizations, especially non-profits, send new leaders off to a one-day session on leadership that is usually held at local hotel or conference center. While this may be a noble effort, it is simply not enough.

New leaders, those who define the future and create a path to get there, and managers, those who make every day effective and efficient, greatly benefit from openly sharing their challenges and learning from one another under the guidance of a seasoned leadership coach.

Seminars and workshops have their place. However, they are usually led by professional presenters who may or may not have a solid and successful track record outside the classroom. Many times, leaders come home overloaded with a lot a great information, but don't have a clue on how to implement it where they are expected to lead real human beings.

Consultants are like doctors. They arrive at the scene, do a thorough assessment, write a prescription that is supposed to fix everything, collect their fee and leave. If that prescription does not work, they always have more as long as you have the money. This is why I'm a huge proponent of group coaching.

That means coming alongside the leader and his or her team for an extended length of time and being brutally honest about their challenges. Then, help them find ways to address the challenges and find out what they do best and do more of it.

I have led these groups myself and can attest to their effectiveness. The investment required for this is significantly less than the cost of one placement fee to replace a core leader who left because his or her "boss" did not have a clue how to lead people.

Talk to your team. Here is an idea that won't cost you a dime. Ask them what their hopes and dreams were when they began working for your organization. Follow up by asking if they still feel this way. If they say no, seek their input in terms of what you can do to change this. Then take action.

Of course, you could choose to sit back as a naive or uninformed leader and enjoy what you believe is the ideal work opportunity and environment.

If you do, don't be surprised when a team member knocks on your office door, envelope in hand, and says, "Got a minute?"

"The most fruitful leadership lessons are not lying around on the ground at the bottom of the tree."

Leadership lessons are learned with every leadership opportunity at every level. Too many want the title and position without paying the price, maintaining a spirit of humility, the key to great leadership.

Many young and/or immature leaders want the fruit of significant leadership influence without climbing the tree. Fruit that falls at your feet is usually rotten and passed over by real fruit pickers and tree climbers. It is the same with leadership development.

If you get leadership influence any other way than climbing the leadership tree through blood, sweat and tears, it shows up often and in so many ways. Leadership seminars, workshops and MBA degrees are the climbing gear, not a substitute for the critical lessons you learn on your climb to the top.

Be like the snail who started his climb up the apple tree when snow was still on the ground. He passed by a worm sitting out the winter in a crevice. The worm said, "There's no fruit up there." The snail replied, "There will be by the time I get there."

Where are you in your climb up the leadership tree?

Never go out on a limb and stay there. Keep climbing until you reach the top of your potential. Do not be weary in your climb and certainly do not be influenced by the "worms" who are satisfied feeding on the inferior fruit at the bottom of the tree, the place where all inferior leaders hang out.

Week 40

"Great leaders know how to deal with their anger."

A guy's car stalled at an intersection causing a chorus of honking horns from behind. He got out, walked calmly to the car behind him and said, "Sorry, I can't get my car started. If you'd like to give it a shot, I'll sit here and honk your horn."

Issues that build character and perseverance in great leaders create vacillation and indifference in poor leaders. Slamming doors, showing rage and storming out of difficult situations are all signs of immature leaders, regardless of how gifted and talented. Not only are they immature, they are counter-productive and neutralize any positive leadership influence you may have with your team.

Two things that will help you deal with personal anger as a leader are commitment and creativity. Real leaders do not quit when things get difficult and challenges overwhelm them. They refuse to get angry at themselves or at those they lead.

An angry leader was talking to his pastor and said, "It must be hard living an exemplary life, handling all those pressures and people waiting for one sign of weakness, so they can pounce on you. How do you handle it?" Smiling, he replied, "I stay home a lot."

That is probably not an option for you and most leaders. You must find a productive way to deal with your frustrations. Most of the anger management tools on the market today require a lot of will power and mature self-management. They may bring some temporary relief and short-term victories. However, only in God's strength will you be able to handle the demands of people, pressures and problems that come constantly your way.

The second thing that will help is creativity. Homer wrote, "Adversity has the effect of eliciting talents which in prosperous circumstances would have lain dormant." Problems will either make you fight back in anger, flee in frustration, or unlock your creativity.

The story's told of a chicken farmer whose land kept flooding and killing his chickens. In his despair he told his wife, "I've had it. I can't afford to buy another place and I can't sell this one. What can I do?" Calmly she replied, "Buy ducks!"

Great leaders minimize their anger by focusing that energy on finding creative ways to solve the issues creating the anger. People are demanding and problems never stop coming. Both are difficult and draining. Anger is a normal response. How you channel that anger determines your maturity as a leader and measures your ability to lead effectively.

Leadership, regardless of venue, is an inherently emotional journey. When you are leading, it is nearly impossible to avoid becoming emotionally invested, not only in outcomes, but in people and processes as well. However, great leaders rise about the passions of the moment and demonstrate maturity.

"Great leadership is keeping your head, while everyone around you is losing theirs."

General Dwight David Eisenhower

Week 41

"Seven reasons why great leaders keep the vision alive."

On December 21, 1620, the pilgrims landed on Plymouth Rock. Full of vision after a three-month crossing of the Atlantic Ocean, they established a town followed by a town council in year two.

In the third year the council wanted to build a road five miles out into the wilderness for westward expansion. However, the townspeople voted it down as a waste of funds. Once able to see across an ocean, twenty-four months later they could not see five miles down the road.

When you are satisfied with where you are, your vision has died, and forward momentum is lost. When you are more energized by managing the present than you are envisioning the future, you have lost your right to lead.

Here are seven reasons why great leaders keep the vision alive:

1. Vision keeps you and your team focused beyond the daily routine and on the dream. It gives significance to every task, every day.

2. A compelling vision removes uncertainty, constant doubt and hesitation about the future.

3. Clarity about the vision speeds decision-making, decisiveness and forward momentum.

4. Vision keeps you determined, but flexible. Able to handle the bumps and delays, while keeping your eyes on the target.

5. Vision infuses your work with energy, enthusiasm and courage. You may get tired outwardly--but never weary inwardly.

6. Vision helps all team members see their connection to the "big picture." Silo building stops and teamwork becomes the order of the day.

7. Vision keeps you growing when the going gets tough, resources are limited, and some of your most loyal team members walk away.

Remember when you and your team could see across oceans? But now you struggle to see five miles down the road.

Your future, and the future of those who you lead, depend on your continuing passion for the dream, even if it is sometimes just five miles down the road.

"The vision is for a future time...if it seems slow in coming, wait patiently, for it will surely take place. It will not be delayed." Habakkuk 2:3 NLT

"Great leaders never quit, they just get a new grip."

Admiral Peary made seven attempts before he became the first man to reach the North Pole. Shackleton failed in 1915 to reach the South Pole and ended up stranded for eight months on their ice-bound ship, The Endurance.

With his ship now crushed by the ice, he and 28 men took their small lifeboats and traveled 350 miles to Elephant Island. Then Shackleton and four men took a 20-foot lifeboat and sailed 800 miles through a hurricane to South Georgia Island looking for a remote whaling station.

Landing on the wrong side of the island they hiked 26 miles over a mountain range in a blizzard in 36 hours to find it. Then he went back to Elephant Island and rescued his remaining crew, not one was lost. Talk about leadership and perseverance, Shackleton has few equals.

Quitting has more to do with who you are than what you are doing, your circumstances, or how limited your resources. I often say, "I love everyone, but I barely love losers." Losers are not people, but attitudes. Winning consistently often requires an attitude adjustment before you see a change in your circumstances.

You can develop new skills to meet new challenges. You can create new methods and find additional resources—but without getting a new grip on your attitude, you seldom win. This is what separates losers from winners.

The Bible says, "So take a new grip with your tired hands which hang down." Hebrews 12:12.

God never fails, but some days you just have to get a new grip on His timeless truths.

"Tiny things many times create big problems."

On December 29, 1972, Eastern Airlines Flight 401, bound to Miami from New York, crashed into the Florida Everglades because of a twelve-dollar light bulb.

As the plane approached Miami the indicator light for the deployment of landing gear failed to come on. The plane circled over the Everglades while the crew tried to figure out the problem.

Either the landing gear was not working, and they had a major problem on their hands, or it was a simple case of a faulty light bulb. When one of the crew members tried to remove the bulb, he found it was stuck and would not come out.

Soon everyone inside the cockpit were so focused on the light bulb that they failed to look up and see they were losing altitude. The plane eventually slammed into the swamp killing almost everyone on board. It is a tragic example of how we can get caught up in the little things and lose sight of where we are going.

There were enough educated, skilled and experienced people in the cockpit that day to fly that plane to its destination safely. However, they were without a leader keeping his focus on the "big picture" and his eye on the goal. All the education, skill and experience in the world meant nothing on that fateful day.

As a senior leader, your job is to assemble the best team possible before you leave the runway. After you are in flight, your job is to watch two critical "indicators" above everything else. First, is the Attitude Meter, it measures the relative position of the nose of the plane to the horizon line. Second, is the Altimeter, it measures how high you are flying.

No matter how high a plane flies, if you do not keep the attitude of the plane above the horizon line, it's just a matter of time and you will crash. It matters little how skilled and talented your team members are if their attitudes are creating tension at best, or worse, havoc in the cockpit.

Great leaders know that their first responsibility is to monitor the "attitude" of the team. Do they have the mind of a winner and the heart of a servant? They know before they maximize the altitude, the team's ability to fly high, they must keep the attitude above the horizon line. They also know that to reverse the order spells certain failure, it is just a matter of time.

Is your team struggling to gain altitude, have more consistent wins? Have you checked all the "big" issues and still something seems to be missing? When was the last time you checked the Attitude Meter of your team?

"It's the little foxes that spoil the vine." Song of Solomon 2:15

"Who do you trust?"

When I grew up in the 50s there was a TV program known as "To Tell the Truth." It featured four celebrities attempting to correctly identify a described contestant with an unusual occupation.

This central character is accompanied by two impostors who pretend to be the central character. The impostors are allowed to lie but the central character is sworn "to tell the truth."

In the past fourteen years, traveling over 250 days per year, I have personally spoken with several thousand leaders at all levels. The subject of trust is a major issue in almost every conversation.

Most people do not feel their leader is an impostor, but many feels their leader struggles with communicating in a style, and at a level they understand.

When trust is present, you cannot contain it. It overflows to every part of the organization. Without it you must have more corporate policemen manning the grapevine. Leaders who want to build and sustain trust must be visible to all stakeholders and available and accountable to their core leaders.

Absentee leaders, or leaders insulated by an assistant, who also functions part-time as a Prussian guard, erodes team spirit and with it, mutual trust.

Building trust requires sharing inside information and including core leaders in decision-making, especially the significant decisions affecting their personal future.

Caution, trusting unproven or inexperienced people can be tantamount to pinning a "kick me" sign on your back. On the other hand, not trusting your proven core leaders diminishes their trust in you and their passion for the mission and vision.

Breaking trust should be addressed immediately and a clear path to restoration established, sooner rather than later. Broken trust never gets better with age. Trust broken the second time should bring an immediate release of the team member, or a resignation by the leader.

The best way to confirm and affirm those whom you trust is their ability to keep a confidence. The best time to assess their trustworthiness is before a situation arises for the need to tell the truth. Never risk your leadership with people you do not trust or with people who don't trust you.

If you have people on your core team that you would not trust with your pin numbers and passwords, why are they still on your team?

"Vision: Is it received, developed or discovered?"

Father Theodore Hesburgh, former president of Notre Dame University said, "Vision is the essence of leadership."

Vision means knowing where you want to go and how to get there. It requires three things: First, your vision must be clear and compelling. Second, it must be articulated well. Third, your team must be excited about pursuing it.

Above all, you must be consistent. No one follows an uncertain or faint trumpet. It is very difficult to sing harmony when you can't hear the lead.

You develop a clear and compelling vision by using one of the following three approaches; you can impose it, buy it, or forge it through consensus.

First, imposing a vision can be either by demand or persuasion. Teledyne founder, Henry Singleton, believes an organization is built around a mind with an idea that's aware of the key issues of his generation.

Great leaders stay ahead of the curve and lead from the future, not to the future. They are educated visionaries, sharpened by their image of the future and guide their organization with confidence and humility.

Poor leaders impose their vision through demands often disguised as motivation, but in reality, is manipulation. Great leaders' cast their vision until it becomes the common vision of the team through communication that is vivid and compelling.

Second, buying a vision. Consultants will happily create a fashionable mission statement that creates a lot of energy but few sustainable results. The problem with these 'off-the-rack' solutions is they are usually so generic they are worthless, regardless of what you pay for it.

Visions cannot be sold like a McDonalds burger or Starbucks latte. They cannot be a Burger King vision where everyone has it their way. Your team and stakeholders know immediately that you are trying to sell them a second-hand, cut-and-paste dream they reject immediately. If they do not, they are naive and of no real value to the team, release them.

Third, forging a vision happens through leadership consensus by encouraging broad contributions in putting flesh on the skeleton you provide. This produces a vision that is the most enduring and effective for long term sustainable results.

At the end of the process you want a vision that is not only compelling but energizes great buy-in by the core leaders and all the stakeholders. You do not forge a vision overnight, it comes through patience, perseverance and passion.

Ask your frontline team members today, "What is our purpose/vision? How does what you do here connect to that on a daily basis?"

If they cannot answer those questions with any kind of certainty, either you need to reconsider your title as their leader, or they need to reconsider their place on the team.

"Five keys to understanding the emotional side of leadership."

Leaders who think they can ignore the emotional component in leadership are either naive, inexperienced, or willfully incompetent.

As a leader, never forget that you are working with emotionally driven people, not unfeeling robots. Leaders who ignore or are dishonest about their emotions are sick and can do a lot of damage unless corrected ASAP.

Here are five keys to help you deal with emotions, your own and those on your team:

1. Healthy leaders identify and constantly monitor their emotions and those of their team. They recognize how their emotions affect their personal leadership style and the emotions of their team greatly affect the outcome of the mission.

2. They regulate their emotions between what makes them tick and what ticks them off. They understand how emotions influence decisions and what moods are best in any given situation. They don't allow others to manipulate their emotions or those of their team.

3. Great leaders use their emotions, positive and negative, to build a productive environment, regardless of the leadership challenge. You cannot do that unless you identify, understand and consistently maintain control over your own emotions.

4. Even good leaders struggle in harnessing their emotions and making positive decisions in difficult situations. Poor leaders only make situations worse because they either deny, ignore, or refuse to change their emotionally immature behavior.

5. Productive leaders are empathizing leaders. They recognize how emotions provide information otherwise unknown. They are able to see every situation through the eyes of others, without bias, before choosing a course of action.

Nurturing people through emotional leadership is a priority of all great leaders. Great leaders go out of their way to genuinely care for those they serve and those who serve them. They show appreciation for every team member and their contribution, no matter how small or seemingly insignificant.

When setting goals, executing strategy, or simply providing daily leadership; great leaders know how to maintain the best emotional interests of every team member at heart without compromising the mission.

Do you know what makes every member on your team tick, what energizes them to show up every day besides the paycheck? Do you know what ticks them off, de-energizes them and makes them look for any excuse not to show up?

People seldom do quit their job. They usually quit their leader because they "feel like" he doesn't understand who they are beyond being just a producer. People and machines both work better with a little attention.

Who needs a little attention on your team today? Ignore it if you want to, but you do it to your own hurt!

"Do you need to change lures on your vision-casting rod?"

Seasoned fishermen know you rarely catch a fish on the first cast or every cast. However, they never seem to tire of casting their lure until they hear those exciting words, "fish on!"

The same is true with great leaders. They never tire of casting the vision until those they lead are passionate, energized and see their personal connection to its fulfillment. Their leadership tackle box is full of "lures" and they change them often until they find the right one.

Here are five keys to help you cast your vision till you the words, "I see it."

1. Never stop focusing on the vision and casting it often. Avoid getting distracted by the details of its pursuit. Only then can you help your team understand their individual connection without compromising your core values.

2. Allow your team to help you in creating the final draft of 'your' vision, or it never becomes 'our' vision. When you do, the team is far more energized and engaged daily. When you do not, you start experiencing most of your personnel problems.

3. Team members stay engaged and motivated when they clearly understand the vision. They believe what they do everyday matters and continually raise the level of expectations for their assignment. This only happens when the vision is clear, compelling and modeled by the leaders.

4. Your role as a leader is helping everyone on the team plan the route and consistently review the progress. Do not leave anyone behind. Those who don't keep up cause most of your problems and soon become 'vision-drainers.'

5. When leading your team; your primary role is inspiring emotional attachment by making the vision attractive and making success visible and attainable until it becomes the driving force behind everyone's effort.

Successful vision casting and landing the 'big one' means everyone knows their role, helps form the vision, participates in its regular review and celebrates every 'win' along the way, big or small.

If you and your core leaders have made the vision clear and compelling, everyone who should be on your team remains committed to its fulfillment. If not, you should help them find a leader with a vision they can support with passion and energy.

Great leaders allow no room for lone rangers, lagers or silo builders. They inspire everyone to keep moving from just agreeing with the vision to aligning their daily efforts and attitude for its success.

Leaders, as long as you don't get weary casting the vision, your team won't get weary helping you make it happen.

Who on your team today seems to have lost their interest and energy for the vision? Could it be because they no longer see the vision being modeled by their leader? Could it be because they no longer see, or maybe never did see, their personal connection to its fulfillment?

When was the last time you changed lures?

"It's my way or the highway, the cause of most workplace tension"

Balancing tension is high on the agenda of every great leader. Every organization has tension. Left alone it quickly dissipates productive energy and sinks team morale through internal conflict.

Among the tension's leaders deal with, two stand out:

First, great leaders know how to generate an internal competitive urge without creating an internal combative spirit. They also know how to channel this energy into productive activities that energize and benefit everyone on the team.

T.E. Lawrence, a British officer, played by Peter O'Toole in the movie "Lawrence of Arabia," was sent to the Middle East in 1916-18 to enlist the Bedouin tribes to fight against the Ottoman Turks controlling the Arabian Peninsula. However, these tribes were as eager to attack each other as they were to fight the Turks.

Lawrence earned his reputation by successfully redirecting the tensions dividing the tribes into a unified fighting force with one goal, defeating the Islamic Turk's desire to control the Middle East and Europe. Redirecting negative energy into productive channels is a daily task for all leaders, but not many do it well.

The second tension leaders must balance is group decision-making versus decisiveness. Shared decision-making is nothing new. Great generals, kings and CEO's have sought the counsel of trusted advisors for centuries. The challenge is, does it mitigate your authority and influence as a leader? It can, and in many cases leads to everyone's second choice and not the best choice.

Poor leaders are often defensive about their decision-making rights. Emotionally mature leaders on the other hand recognize the benefit of seeking wise counsel, having their assumptions challenged and hearing alternatives. Mature and experienced leaders maximize group input instead of demanding the team accept their edicts without question.

Great leaders don't go it alone, they challenge the team to address unresolved issues. Instead of saying; "Here are the cuts that must be made," they say, "Our task today is determining the best way to balance the budget, given our present reality. Tell me your thoughts, the facts that support them and their likely consequences."

Still, there are times decisions must be made by a process rather than group consensus. Especially in times of crisis or a time crunch. Unilateral decisions by a trusted leader are accepted and supported by even the most critical team members if they are rare and not a way of life.

Great leaders constantly work on balancing the "tension of two truths." Meaning, for every truth there is an opposite and equal truth that keeps them both in tension. For every decision you made there were probably a hundred others you could have made.

With poor leaders it's, "My way or the highway!" With great leaders it's, "Let's find the best way!" If your team could vote anonymously about your decision-making style and skill, how would they vote? Are you sure? Why not ask them?

"Are you determined to win, or just satisfied to compete?"

At Disney, leadership is not defined by your title or position, it is defined by your actions. Every leader proactively works to align their personal values and daily work ethic with the Disney vision and values. Result? A motivated, innovative and productive team.

All leaders are expected to serve as role models for the next generation of leaders. They are told, the WAY you lead tells a story about your values and contributes to the leadership legacy at the world's number one entertainment company.

Team members who are satisfied with average at best, or worse, mediocre, are a threat to any team that wants to excel.

Winning, depending on how you keep score, may not be everything but not doing your best all the time is a weakness great leaders will not tolerate. The moment you settle for second best you are no longer an asset but a liability the rest of the team must carry.

As a leader you not only have to manage your own expectations of winning, but also those of your team. You must face every challenge with the determination to win. Over time, your determined expectations must affect everyone on the team, or you forfeit your right to lead.

If anyone on the team is more determined to win than you, they should be leading, not you. You do not have to be the best at every task, however, you should have no peers when it comes to passion or determination.

There are no excuses for lack of determination in a leader. If you believe in the mission then it is worthy of everyone's best efforts, especially yours as the leader. Passionate determination differentiates average leaders from great leaders, and it must be nurtured and invigorated constantly.

No one can predict the future but determined leaders can be counted on to lead the way with above average courage and determination until victory is assured. Lack of passionate determination to win should disqualify any leader.

Abraham Lincoln said, "Everything comes to those who wait but only things left by those who hustle."

You either lead with determination and find a way to win, or you learn to accept the leftovers of those who hustle.

Which leader would you follow? Why do people follow you? Because you are a winner, or because you are satisfied coming in second?

"Carrots, do they help or hinder?"

Great leaders know shaping an inspirational and motivational workplace is the only way to sustain superior performance and achieve above average results. This is best accomplished through self-motivated team members, not external rewards or bonuses.

Everyone likes to be recognized and rewarded. When handing out rewards keep the following three things in mind:

First, inappropriate or ill-timed rewards consistently undermine sustained, long-term motivation and performance. While rewards give a temporary boost, motivation generally falls off sharply once people receive the reward and wait for the next one. Great team members do not want or need rewards to control their environment or increase their efforts.

Second, offering rewards for something team members already enjoy doing many times undermines motivation and weakens performance. Often rewards turn self-satisfying opportunities into real 'work.'

Great team members appreciate rewards but would give the same effort without them. Poor attitudes and work ethics are never overcome by rewards. Most of the time they are only made worse.

Third, rewards often make it difficult for team members to be creative and solve complex problems. Incentivizing creativity, especially to meet deadlines, actually slows progress due to pressure and stress.

External rewards narrow their focus to a drive to the finish line closing off new connections and opportunities so vital to creativity. Excessive rewarding many times leads to unethical behavior instead of creative problem solving.

Poor leaders try to motivate inferior team members through a reward system. Great leaders give recognition, verbal and written, acknowledging true individual or team results.

Offering personal recognition takes reflection, observation and regularity. However, in the end it addresses the felt needs of your team members producing quality and sustainable results, not a temporary spike in behavior caused by an impersonal reward system.

When was the last time you went out of your way to personally recognize the team members who make you look good? Carrots are helpful and appreciated, but nothing takes the place of a sincere "thank you"!

Week 51

"If you want to win--get the right people on your team."

Stop looking for the 'best' and most talented people, look for the right people. It is a waste of time to talk vision, leadership and strategy with people who are a not a good fit for your team, regardless of their talent, ability and past success on other teams.

Keep three things in mind when you are looking for future team members:

1. VISION: chasing an awesome dream with the wrong people can soon turn into a nightmare for many reasons. Lack of servant-driven leadership is at the top of the list.

2. PEOPLE DEVELOPMENT: a stronger whip won't move a dead horse, and more carrots won't energize an apathetic team member. You need to find out what makes future team members tick and what ticks them off before they join your team

3. STRATEGY: an "A" strategy executed by a "C" team would be comical if it were not so pathetic. Passionate pursuit of a great action plan with the wrong team just means you get to failure quicker.

Great leaders never forget that you teach people to know, you train them to perform, and you inspire them to action. They only recruit people of proven character, integrity and loyalty that possess the mind of a winner and the heart of a servant to join their team. To do otherwise, they know means setting themselves up for disappointment.

Take a look at your team. Who's struggling, but still worth the investment of your time, energy and resources? Who needs released, so they can find a team where they would be a better fit?

The sooner you answer these two questions with brutal honesty, exercise the courage to make the appropriate decisions, no matter how tough, the sooner you will have a winning team!

"Why the good ones leave you."

Finding good team members is hard, finding the few great ones even harder. Keeping the good ones is what separates great leaders from all the rest. Keeping the great ones is rare, even for the best of leaders.

Few people quit their job or place of service, they quit their leader. Your team turnover rate is always a good indicator of how well you attract, develop, and retain good people and future leaders.

Great leaders and healthy organizations are always ahead of the learning curve in retaining the good ones for the long haul. Great people come and go, but if good people are leaving frequently, consider the following:

First, did you fail the 'what makes them tick' test? They are bored and under challenged. You should have handled that in the performance agreement when they joined your team. If you didn't, it's never too late.

Second, did you fail the, 'what ticks them off' test? You do not allow them creative and innovative license. Give them a challenge, agree on the expectations, then get out of their way and become their biggest cheerleader.

Third, did you continue their personal growth and career development? This is not about the annual review addressing their past year's performance, but succession planning and their future career advancement, not yours.

Fourth, did you make the emotional connection? Good people want more than a professional relationship. This is not about being best buddies. However, sincere and respectful friendships never hurt and usually pay great dividends.

Fifth, did you adequately recognize and reward their contribution? They may brush it off in conversation, but people and machines still work better with a little attention. Recognition must be timely, intentional and personal.

Sixth, did you fail to increase their organizational footprint through wider visibility and greater responsibilities? All great performers want to have more influence on their own and the organization's future.

Seventh, did you keep your promises? Don't promise more than you can deliver, but don't fail to promise. Always under promise and over deliver. Asking forgiveness is one thing, earning back trust quite another. Second chances are rare, and the relationship is seldom the same.

If you follow these seven principles you make it very painful for good people to leave you, regardless of what others may offer them.

Benefits and value of Executive Leadership Coaching with Dr. David Robinson

His coaching is highly relational. The content is executive level and relevant. However, the real value is the relationship and accessibility to him as your personal coach.

Dr. Robinson's wisdom and experience is invaluable given his leadership experience at all levels in both the Church world and the Marketplace since 1966.

He focuses on five things:

1. Clarifying your mission, vision, values and strategy.
2. Finding out what you do best, a way to more of it and way to do it better.
3. Sorting through all of your opportunities, prioritizing and then focusing on those giving you the greatest return on the investment of your time, energy and resources.
4. Determining specific and strategic action steps that help you and your team reach your goals, execute your strategy and advance your vision.
5. Achieving balance in your life while accomplishing your personal, family and vocational goals.

He does not charge for his services. However, he does ask for a monthly donation to City Limits International Ministries for his missions' work.

For complete bio and how you can benefit from using him as a coach for your church, business, government service or in the educational field please visit: www.coaching4ministers.com

You can contact him at c4mcoach@gmail.com.

Thousands of people have already used the principles in this book to improve their leadership skills, and see results. Now it's your turn!

I call you blessed!

[signature]

The Coach

NOTES

NOTES

NOTES

NOTES

Made in the USA
Columbia, SC
03 October 2020